OBSERVATIONS FROM THE WEIRD BEARDED GUY

A Collection of Thoughts, Insights, and Words of Encouragement.

By Mike Gilbert

PublishAmerica
Baltimore

© 2008 by Mike Gilbert.
All rights reserved. No part of this book may be reproduced, stored in a retrieval system or transmitted in any form or by any means without the prior written permission of the publishers, except by a reviewer who may quote brief passages in a review to be printed in a newspaper, magazine or journal.

First printing

PublishAmerica has allowed this work to remain exactly as the author intended, verbatim, without editorial input.

ISBN: 1-60703-062-4
PUBLISHED BY PUBLISHAMERICA, LLLP
www.publishamerica.com
Baltimore

Printed in the United States of America

FOREWORD

I like to laugh, I've learned to love, and I love to encourage.

So, it's no surprise that I find humor in observing people—all kinds of people. I have found that God's sense of humor is present and visible if we look hard enough to see how He has uniquely created each individual: fat, skinny, short, or tall, people of all races and nationalities, "children" of all ages, of both genders, religious or non-religious, hairy or hairless, smooth shaven or bearded, articulate or mute, rural or city folk, educated or illiterate, sophisticate or rube, Democrat, Republican, Libertarian, Independent, Socialist, or apolitcal, conservative or liberal, pro-life or pro-choice, introvert or extrovert, meat eater or vegetarian, boomer or buster, Gen-X or greatest generation, leader or follower, prim and proper or loosey-goosey, dog lover or cat person, rock 'n roller or Conway Twitty fan. What a great mix. What a funny bunch. What a creative Creator.

I'm also very much a skeptic, a satirist, and teacher.

Raised in the "Show Me" state of Missouri, I'm not easily convinced that things are always as they are presented. I like to poke, jab, dig, and "test" the spirits to see if they are genuine, or, as they say in the Ozarks, "the real McCoy."
When, after my own "research," I find them to be genuine, I love to teach others the truths I've discovered. But when I discover things to be incongruous to their claims of legitimacy, as a satirist I love to point out those inconsistencies also.

Finally, I'm a "big picture" kind of guy.

I like to look past the here and now, past the intricate details of events, and see how the events "fit in" as part of the "big picture" of life. I have found it important to step back, zoom out, and see each day's events as part of the quilt of our lives, part of God's unfolding plan, and then to apply the truths we find to helping us live better, more meaningful lives tomorrow.

Hence, this is a book of some of my observations.

I have collected them over the years, mentioned a few of them now and then, but mostly kept them pretty close to the vest. However, after the encouragement of many, I have put them in book form and hope you will be encouraged by them.

At the close of each observation, I've attached a "To the reader" section, offering my hope of what you might glean from that observation. Of course, you're free to glean whatever you see, collect your own observations. However, I hope this section will serve to encourage you to look within at your own life and how this particular observation might collide or cohere to your own, and might help you expand or clarify your own perspective, your own "take" on the event and thoughts I've expressed.

Likewise, the "To the Lord" section is an expression of my gratitude to the Lord for what He taught me as I experienced and/or "researched" the topic of that observation.

Allow me to say, 'Thanks."

Many people have played a part in bringing this book into being.

To my wife, Becky, and my now-grown children, Kim and Jeff, thank you for putting up with my ramblings, my incessant questioning of authority and trying to see inside and
pierce through the events of each day, seeking to glean meaning and perspective. I'm sure it wasn't always fun for you, and although I think our culture has given the idea of "tolerance" a much too elevated position, this is one case where your tolerance should be applauded. So I applaud you, and I thank you, and I love you.

To my parents, Nolan and Donna Gilbert, thank you for allowing me the freedom to think my own thoughts, explore the world of ideas and viewpoints, and come to my own conclusions. Thank you for guiding me in grounding and basing my life on God's Word, for serving as examples of persons being always ready to learn something new, to challenge the status quo (which is many times nothing to "quo" about), and to unashamedly stand for what is right, regardless of how many others might opt for that which is merely convenient or popular.

To the thousands of teenagers I have had the joy and privilege of serving, teaching, and learning from, thank you. Becky and I still lift you up in our prayers and wish you the very best of life.

To the staff members, church members, and students who endured the numerous meetings, sermons, and college classes, thank you for your patience, insights and encouragements along the way. As I was seeking to bless your lives you have been such a blessing to mine.

Yet, my greatest thanks is to You, Lord. I will never be able to say thank You enough. Thank You for the good times, the laughs, and the blessings. Thank You for the peace only You can give, for forgiveness and grace, and for helping me learn that as complicated as life might seem, sometimes, if you look at it all in the right way, there is a plan, an order, and a simplicity that can be observed. Thank You not only for the good times, though. I thank You too for the difficult times You allowed me to come through; they served to prove to me Your faithfulness, that You are indeed in charge at all times, and that sometimes we can only appreciate simplicity after we've experienced and come to grips with that which is complicated. My prayer is that this book, merely a collection of what You have led me to observe and learn from, will somehow serve to bring You glory and might also be a blessing to others as they read it, ruminate on the observations, and perhaps be challenged by some of them. Glorifying You, Lord, is, in fact, my sole reason for putting pen to these observations. So, it's Yours, Lord. Use it as You wish.

And thanks again.

TABLE OF CONTENTS

THE BARKING BOY AND THE WINNING GOAL	9
LIFE IS SO DAILY	11
THE ROCK 'N ROLL HALL OF FAME	13
"THEE" GAME ON SUNDAYS	15
THE LEADING CAUSE OF DEATH	18
CORRECTNESS RUN AMOK	20
LIFE ACCORDING TO GUMP	22
MORE THAN EGGS ON EASTER	25
ENDING THE UNDECLARED WAR	27
THE GOLDEN CALF…Uhh, PARLOR	30
THE CASE OF THE CUSTOM-MADE EAR PLUGS	33
COMMENCEMENT	35
RIGHT MOTIVE, WRONG METHOD	38
REAL MEN GROW UP	40
LOST, FOUND, REJOICING	43
WHAT'S RIGHT WITH AMERICA	45
THE DISGUISE OF ACTIVITY	47
DOING "THE WAVE"	49
ANIMALS GONE WILD!	51
THE CARPENTER DOES BATHROOMS TOO	53
CHEER UP!	56
LOVE BRACELETS	59
PRECIOUS MEMORIES	61
LOVE IN ACTION	63
WALKS LIKE A DUCK, QUACKS LIKE A TURKEY	65
VANITY, VANITY	67
SAME MESSAGE, VERY DIFFERENT CROWDS	69

BAPTIZED IN THE JORDAN 71
NO DUTCH TREAT 73
TWELVE PARTRIDGES AND TWELVE PEAR TREES 75
'TWAS THE NIGHT BEFORE CHRISTMAS 77
AN EPILOGUE 80
NOTES 82

THE BARKING BOY AND THE WINNING GOAL

It was one of those times when I laughed so hard it actually hurt.

I've seen the replay about twenty times as television sportscasters focused on their traditional "end of the year" remembrances, but that first time was the funniest by far.

The scene was nothing really out of the ordinary at first: it was a typical winter Friday night somewhere in the rural Midwest, which meant the focus of their small town was on the high school basketball game. And, it was not all that unusual to have a one-point difference in the score with only a few seconds remaining in the game.

However, from there the scene moved from the sublime to the ridiculous...

As the home team prepared to toss the ball in from just under their own basket, their point guard suddenly moved clear to the far corner of the court, fell down on all fours...and began BARKING LIKE A DOG!

The visiting team, completely distracted, shifted their attention to the barking boy and FORGOT that the outcome of the game was being decided. They were caught off-guard as the home team then passed the ball, uncontested, to their star center who was standing just inches away from the basket, and who easily made the lay-up that won the game!

Needless to say, the place went berserk. The barking boy quickly jumped up and assumed his normal two-legged posture, then joined the rest of his team, coaches, cheerleaders, and fans who had now mobbed the court, jumping and shouting and celebrating their surprise victory over their distracted opponents!

Funny, isn't it?

However, it's only funny because it concerns something so eternally inconsequential as a basketball game.

It's not truly funny when it happens, as it does every day, in the "game" of life, where not basketball games but souls are at stake.

As a born again Christian, I've been instructed by my Savior to "keep the main thing the main thing," being a faithful messenger of the gospel, telling others in words and also by my actions about Jesus, His love, His forgiveness, His grace, His power, and His soon return. And yet, if I'm not careful and properly focused I can become distracted by the lures and wiles of the world. Instead of keeping my head in the game, if I'm not careful I'll start watching "players" who are crawling around and barking like dogs.

To the reader…

I invite you to "get in the game" by receiving Jesus today, and no longer listen to the "hound" of hell. You'll be glad you did, and, believe me, this is no game…your very life and soul are at stake.

To the Lord…

Thanks for passing to me Your forgiveness, Your promises, Your presence, and for making me a part of Your winning team. Help me to keep in mind the fact that You've already scored the winning goal, and I can now celebrate.

LIFE IS SO DAILY

In his book, Starting Over,[1] Chuck Swindoll tells about his boyhood vacations in South Texas. One such summer while spending some time at his grandfather's cottage near the Gulf of Mexico, young Chuck began talking with his grandfather's African American cook, Coats. Coats was a friendly and unique gentleman who began to give Chuck a vivid account of some of the ups and downs life had handed him.

Finally, the thoughtful and caring hired hand knelt down to the lad's height and simply but profoundly explained, "Charles, the hardest thing about life is that it's so daily."[2]

No truer words have ever been spoken. And yet, I thank God that it is so because there is much hope in the fact that life is lived not in the long-term so much, but lived one day at a time.

Just think of the benefits of living life one day at a time…
* We don't have to carry more than a day's load at any time.
* We get to start over, fresh and new, each day.
* The Lord's mercies are new and fresh each day also.
* Each day we're one day closer to seeing the Lord's face.

I often ask folks to work together in a group "think tank" in making decisions based on a hypothetical case: Suppose you were given $86,400 today to spend any way you choose, with another $86,400 being given to you again tomorrow, the same the next day, the same for a total of seven days, a full week, what would you do with the sum you were given? Oh, by the way, there is a stipulation: whatever you don't spend today will disappear at the stroke of midnight, never to be seen again, so it must be invested or spent in something, not merely tucked away under your mattress.

It has been interesting over the years to see how groups and individuals decide to "spend" their "money." Try it if you'd like. Of course, it's hypothetical. No one is going to come along and hand you $86,400 today, let alone seven days in a row; sorry to burst your bubble. (It was fun dreaming awhile though, wasn't it?)

However, in the past twenty four hours you HAVE been handed 86,400 seconds. Once they passed they are seconds you will never again see. How well did you spend them?

You see, the hardest thing about life is that it is so daily. The good news is that today is another day. How's it going so far? Are you spending today's 86,400 seconds wisely?

By the way, have you bothered to thank God for giving you 86,400 seconds in the first place, for giving you another day of life? And, carrying it further, let me ask you a final question: does it seem like you might be trying to carry more than one day's load?

You see, life is indeed daily, but so is God's love. His love, His presence, and His help is enough to bring you through your darkest day, enough to shed hope on tomorrow, and more than enough to handle whatever load you're carrying.

To the reader...
How about it? Will you give over your load to Jesus...today?

To the Lord...
Help me remember that today is the day You have made, and help me to rejoice and be glad in it!

THE ROCK 'N ROLL HALL OF FAME

Two months ago Corey, bassist for the Allman Brothers Band was indicted for drug possession. Yet, last night he was inducted into the Rock 'n Roll Hall of "Fame."
So too, was Frank Zappa.
Three years ago, during Congressional hearings concerning parental labeling of rock lyrics, Zappa called anyone who believed that Jesus was more than a teacher "demented."[3] Yet, last night this avant-garde "champion" of the anti-establishment manifesto became a post-mortem inductee into the "establishment" of rock history. Interestingly, there were no cries of hypocrisy from his daughter, Moon Unit Zappa, although had anyone of the pro-life cause been part to such a farce you can bet she would have been publicly vocal in pointing out such a discrepancy.

Other inductees last night included Led Zeppelin (who claim their music is best appreciated when you're high and whose greatest hit was the drug-related Stairway To Heaven[4]), Neil Young (self-confessed "fried" doper who now touts the "glory and wonders" of New Age and thoughts of reincarnation), and Janis Joplin (the self-proclaimed Mama of Soul who committed suicide rather than face her drug addiction and the stresses of broken relationships in the late 1960's), as well as some others.

In response, I offer instead the following individuals introduced to us in the Bible as being more proper inductees into the rock 'n roll Hall of Fame...

a) Simon Peter.

His actual name was Cephas ("little pebble") so he's a logical choice for the "rock" hall. But, more importantly, he learned to "roll" with the punches...whether thrown into prison, ridiculed, or put into delicate and difficult situations like being called to testify before the Council of Jerusalem. Still, even when facing his own crucifixion he remained "solid" by relying on the Holy Spirit.

b) King David.

The first and perhaps greatest stringed instrument player of all time, his music soothed his king, and many of his songs, including some that advocated using loud drums in accompaniment (as in Psalm 150) are still sung thousands of years later after they became the basis for the largest book in the Bible, the Psalms. On top of all of that, he was really great with rock: he sailed one of them right between Goliath's eyes, and moments later, the giant's head rolled! He actually qualifies for a lot of different Halls, especially the Hall of Faith, recognizing those who had a heart for God and were willing to obey Him, no matter what.

c) All true believers.

Why? Because our feet are on the Rock (Jesus, the Solid Rock), our names are on the roll (the Lamb's Book of Life), and we've been given the greatest name of all…Christians!

To the reader…

Today I encourage you to come to Jesus, the Rock Who doesn't roll, avoiding (coining the lyrics of also-inducted Martha and the Vandellas[5]) an eternal "heat wave."

To the Lord…

Thanks for giving me the courage to march to a different drummer.

"THEE" GAME ON SUNDAYS

"THE Game" is being played today. Some call it a Super game, it certainly has been super-hyped. But if the truth were told, "THEE Game" is played every Sunday…in church.

"Thee Game," just like the Super Bowl, has a vocabulary of terms. Today, if you happen to be watching as guys wearing tight pants and jerseys pass a pigskin back and forth, you might hear some of the same vocabulary utilized in "Thee Game," so I thought I'd put together a brief lexicon to help you in understanding the terms and being able to better observe "Thee Game" with a more expert eye.

Here are a few of the terms you might hear:
a) An End Around.
    This is sometimes a necessary maneuver in worship caused by regular attendees sitting right on the aisle, forcing guests or late-comers to do an "end around" in order to find a place to sit.
b) The Nickel Defense.
    This is a common "defense" used by some to ward off evil spirits or "cover" themselves from bad things happening in their lives: they simply put a nickel or some other small sum (any amount less than ten percent of one's income, qualifies) in the offering plate. This, by the way, was developed by someone whose life soon became a disaster.
c) The Two Minute Warning.
    This is a reminder given by the Music Minister to the ushers that we're getting ready to sing the offertory song today, so they need to get their plates in hand, and get into their proper places in order to receive today's offering.

d) The End Zone.

This is the part of a person's anatomy that can become sore when the sermon goes too long. (Fortunately this is a malady that seems to be reserved primarily for folk in other divisions or conferences, certainly never here where the weird bearded guy is preaching!…Cough…gag…Sorry.)

e) Personal Foul.

This offense occurs most times at church pot-lucks, as in the case of one person saying to another, "Hey, that's my chicken! Don't take that foul off of my plate!"

f) Unnecessary Roughness.

This is the haphazard, disjointed result of a soloist, musician, worship leader, or preacher who hasn't spent enough time preparing for what they are going to sing, play, or preach on Sunday morning.

g) An All-Out Blitz.

A description of the congregation heading for restaurants immediately following the worship service.

h) A Quarterback Sneak.

Related to the all-out blitz, this maneuver is implemented by a person who sits one quarter of the distance from the back pew to the exit door so as to "sneak out" during the invitation or closing prayer, thus getting a head start on the rest of the restaurant-seeking congregation and public.

i) Touch Down!

This wonderful event is when God's Holy Spirit reaches down and touches the hearts of those who are worshipping Him. The result is a changed life, and…

j) An Interception.

This most blessed occurrence during "Thee Game" is when God intervenes and intercepts a person who was headed for hell, saves their soul, and turns their life around the other direction. You see, THIS is what is truly Super!

To the reader…
How is your "game," your life today?
Have you experienced God's interception?
Would you like for Him to touch down in your heart today?

OBSERVATIONS FROM THE WEIRD BEARDED GUY

He's ready to make you a champion, my friend.

To the Lord…
Thank You that when my sin was passed to You, You didn't fumble it, but won the game for me.

THE LEADING CAUSE OF DEATH

The government's Bureau of Statistics, in conjunction with the American Medical Association, announced a few years ago its "official" report, declaring at that time that A.I.D.S had become the number one killer of adults between the ages of 25 and 45.

I know the A.M.A. is a reputable group, and I believe their intentions are honorable. They're attempting to bring our attention to a disease many would rather not hear about, believing it to be too "seedy" to discuss in public, but all need to be aware of. And, the Bureau of Statistics is admirably attempting to warn us and make us aware of the risks and danger inherent in engaging in activities which lend themselves to acquiring H.I.V. and having it "bloom" into full-blown A.I.D.S.

However, as honorable as their intentions are, I disagree with their findings.

No, I don't dispute the Bureau's stats (they reported that A.I.D.S. was claiming the life of 35 out of every 10,000 young adults), and I don't dispute their truly sad disclosure that A.I.D.S.-related deaths had reached the point where they exceeded the number of deaths caused by automobile accidents for this age group.

What I dispute is their "ranking" of A.I.D.S. as the number one killer. You see, I know of a killer with a much higher and much more "deadly" death rate than A.I.D.S. Ironically, just mentioning it is likely to result in jeering or taunting aimed at the person bold enough to speak its deadly name in public, or elicit cries from many amounting to an open denial concerning the very existence of such a killer. And, whereas the President and Congress will grant billions of dollars this year to A.I.D.S. research, absolutely NO Congressional funding will be directed to "combat" and proclaim publicly the cure for this most deadly of all killers:

OBSERVATIONS FROM THE WEIRD BEARDED GUY

SIN.

Yes, you heard me right…sin.

Although most folk don't want to talk about sin anymore, preferring to "keep it in the closet" so as not to disturb those who might be offended by its discussion, the truth is that

SIN LEFT "UNTREATED" KILLS 100% OF THE POPULATION.

That's right…10,000 out of every 10,000 will die from sin left untreated. The apostle Paul, in the book of Romans, tells us both the fatality rate AND the cure for this number one cause of death among Americans and folk of all nations, ages, genders, and orientations. "For ALL have sinned (Rom.3:23)…" and "the wages (result) of sin is DEATH (Rom.6:23)."

In other words, the casualty rate is 100%, and the results are fatal!

Yet, the last half of Romans 6:23 presents the cure, explaining… "but the free gift of God is eternal life though Christ Jesus our Lord."

God's amazing grace shines through, for where there is a 100% death rate for sin, God provides a 100% cure-rate for those who will RECEIVE the cure, for those who receive Jesus as Savior and Lord.

So, today I'm asking you:
    Which group are YOU in?
    Are you DYING in your sin, or are you ALIVE in Christ?
    Have you received the cure, have you confessed your sin and turned from your sinful ways, turning to Jesus and receiving Him by faith for the forgiveness of your sin and for receiving, through Him, by gift of everlasting life with Him?

To the reader…
    If you haven't yet, I implore you: please receive the cure. You don't have to die.
    By receiving Jesus you'll also enjoy life to the fullest, a life empowered by the One Who created life in the first place.

To the Lord…
    Thank you for providing me the Cure for sin.
    Now, Lord, I could use a little help with my driving too.

CORRECTNESS RUN AMOK

The keynote event occurred at the very dawn of the "be sensitive or else" nineties, when the New York State courts granted Donna Ellen Cooperman the right to be known as Donna Ellen CooperPERSON.[6]

Unfortunately, though, the quest of some to thrust their "gospel" of political correctness upon us is far from over. A friend recently loaned me her copy (she bought it thinking it was a joke, but soon learned it was not) of The Official Politically Correct Dictionary and Handbook, from which I have gleaned a few phrases to help all of us. I'm sure you'll be ever-so-delighted to be so enlightened now.

As to animals...

* Pets are no longer to be called pets, they are "nonhuman companions" and frozen chickens purchased at the supermarket are now "voiceless victims of speciesism."

* Zoo keepers or zoo guides are "wildlife presentation center docents."

* From now on a fish in U. S. waters is to be known as an "ichthio-American, just like a puppet is now a "hand-held American."

As to people...

* Handicapped folk are actually "handi-capable," just as deaf or hearing impaired persons are merely "aurally inconvenienced."

* Bald persons are "hair disadvantaged," short people are "vertically disadvantaged."

* What was once known as appearing in public during a "bad hair day" is now called being a "lookism survivor."

* Senior adults aren't aging or mature any longer, they are simply "chronologically challenged," while younger folk are no longer to be referred to as boys and girls but rather as "pre-men" and "pre-women."

My favorites in this tripe, however, include the "spontaneous display of community dissatisfaction with prevailing socioeconomic conditions" (formerly known as a riot), created after the Rodney King verdict at which point looters became "nontraditional shoppers!" Imagine their audacity: they didn't even bother to put their "temporarily repositioned materials" (stolen goods) into "processed tree carcasses" (paper bags)![7]

Well, my friend, even though the phrases I'm about to use are NOT politically correct or popular, nevertheless they are true: Jesus loves you—as the special and unique individual you are—and He demonstrated His great love by leaving His home in heaven to take your place on an old wooden cross, dying that you might be forgiven, and rising from the dead that you might live eternally.

To the reader…
    The most "correct" thing you could ever do would be to receive Him by faith as Savior and Lord.
    Will you today?

To the Lord…
    Thank You, Jesus, that You're not "terminally inconvenienced" (dead), but "metabolically abled" (alive), and You are forever Lord ("Master," God)!

LIFE ACCORDING TO GUMP

Although movie theaters are very rarely the site where profound Biblical truths are presented, there has been one glaring exception recently, a flick that graced millions of theater screens and some profound truth nuggets were uttered from the lips of a very unlikely source…FORREST GUMP![8]

Understand, I'm neither promoting the movie nor claiming it is entirely a theological film. Although poignant in places, it is actually a slick picture of farce and fiction geared to be humorous rather than thought-provoking.

Yet, from the mouth of Forrest Gump's mom or from Forrest himself come the following four "Gump-isms" the Bible agrees with in principle:

#1—"Life is like a box of chocolates; ya never know what you're gonna get."

This most-quoted Gumpism is very true.

The Bible tells us to take no thought for tomorrow because we don't even know what today holds, let alone tomorrow or the future. We're told it rains on the just and the unjust, that sometimes God allows a thorn for some while healing others, etc. One man was even called a fool for planning to build bigger barns to hold all his wealth when what he didn't know was that his life would be taken away the very next day.

However, we do know Who it is Who holds tomorrow, and we can claim God's promise that all things will work together for the good to those who love God and are His children, called according to His purpose. That much we do know, and can count on it.

#2—"Stupid is as stupid does."

Well, I don't believe we should ever call anyone "stupid," but the idea that we demonstrate who we are by our actions is very Biblical.

Faith without works is dead. So…faithful is as faithful does! Walking the walk is the true measure of faith, not just talking the talk. We're reminded that we will know a person by their fruit (their deeds).

#3—"Death is a part of life."

The good news of the gospel is that everlasting life is available through receiving Jesus as Lord and Savior by faith. Therefore, death for a Christian is simply a change of location, not a change of existence. We are reminded in Scripture that to be absent from the body (being physically dead) is to be present with the Lord (for a Christian) or to be immediately in hell (for the non-believer).

So, in that way death is indeed a part of life because where we will spend eternity can only be decided while we're alive on the earth.

My favorite Gumpism, however, is number four. To understand it, though, we need to go back to the context from which it came: six-year old Forrest, handicapped with leg braces, mildly retarded but very loving, on his very first day of riding a school bus, is turned down by everyone on the bus for a seat except one little girl, Jenny, who later will become his life-long friend and eventually his wife. Jenny tells Forrest, "Hi, my name is Jennifer, but people call me Jenny," to which Forrest answers:

#4—"My name is Forrest Gump; people call me Forrest Gump."

Forrest is a young man who never tries to be anyone he isn't, and, as a result, is recognized for being someone very special—simply Forrest Gump.

To some people Forrest might appear "stupid" but Forrest refuses that label or any other, and is content to be exactly who God made him to be.

That's exactly how we are to be too. The only "image" that truly matters is how we appear in our Heavenly Father's eyes. And, for believers, we are forgiven sinners—nothing more, nor less. And behold, "it is very good."

To the reader…

Today I ask you this question: "Who are YOU?"

You see, regardless of what others might call you, God made you, and He doesn't make any junk!

And, God loves you. He sent His Son to save you from the penalty of your sin.

So today I challenge you: be who God made you to be by receiving Jesus and then let Him lead your life. You'll be glad you did.

To the Lord…

Thank You for giving me life…and also for the chocolates!

MORE THAN EGGS ON EASTER

On this Easter Sunday, as our hearts focus on the tremendous gifts Jesus made available to us: forgiveness, a relationship with Him, and everlasting life…all free of charge to us, paid for by His own blood which resulted in His own death, and secured by His glorious resurrection, I'm reminded of the true story of Mr. Ward and Tony.

I'm not sure where or from what source I first heard of the story, and have unsuccessfully tried to find the source, but the events unfolded as follows…

Mr. Ward, a wealthy industrialist of a time gone by, stopped by every morning at a certain shoeshine parlor (see, I told you it was a time gone by), where a young Italian boy, Tony, always shined his shoes. The two developed a friendship over the years and one morning Ward asked his young friend, "Tony, if you could have one wish fulfilled, what would that wish be?"

Tony stopped, looked his friend in the eye, and replied unhesitatingly, "I would like to study medicine. Above everything else in the world, I would like to be a doctor…but I have to take care of my mother."

Deeply moved by Tony's commitment and desire, the philanthropist then asked, "Tony, suppose I told you that I would like to GIVE you…not lend you…enough money to send you through the university and medical school, what would you say?"

Smiling slightly, the boy answered, "I'd say you wouldn't do it."

"I will do it, Tony. You are shining your last pair of shoes."

At this, with tears running down his cheeks, Tony laid down the shoe shine rag and kissed Ward's shoes, bathing them with his tears.

Their friendship continued while arduous years of schooling were completed. Time passed. Soon Tony married and began enjoying a very lucrative medical practice.

One day a beautiful new car stopped in front of Mr. Ward's executive office. Young doctor Tony hurried up the familiar stairway and greeted his benefactor in a tender way. Finally, Doctor Tony said, "This is a great day for me, Mr. Ward. Here's a check, reimbursing you for all the money you have spent on my education…with interest."

Ward quietly took the check, looked at it for a brief moment, then slowly endorsed it and handed it back to a stunned Tony.

"Tony," Ward explained, "I never expect any returns from investments I make in human lives. Besides, God has already credited me with it on His books, so this money really doesn't belong to me at all. I encourage you to take and find ANOTHER BOY that is worthy. Send him through school on it, and maybe someday he will hand it back to you."

You see, that is the true spirit of Easter.

God gave His Son to be born of a young Jewish virgin, to spend thirty years in preparation for three years of ministry, to preach the Gospel of God's grace, the good news of God's redemption and forgiveness offered to those who receive Him. This Son, Jesus, then completed His mission by willfully laying down His own life as payment for others' sins. Asking no favors nor privileges, He died among criminals even though He never sinned

And what does He ask us to do about it in return? Two things:

a) Receive His gift freely by faith.

b) Then, once we've received it, and benefited from it, He wants us to give it away to someone else…equally free.

To the reader…

My single wish today is that you might receive Jesus.

I recommend Him to you freely and prayerfully, because I want you to also experience, as I have, the benefits and joy that only He can bring.

To the Lord…

Please help me to give others Your gift…so much greater than a basketful of colored eggs or a chocolate bunny.

ENDING THE UNDECLARED WAR

This week marks the 30th anniversary of the day when the last of our troops and American personnel left the jungles of Vietnam, marking the "official" end of America's involvement in the Vietnam police action (it was never actually declared a war).

Yet, the truth is: It's not truly ended...because humans are involved.

Some consequences are inevitable, but some exist by choice.
Regardless of whether we might agree or disagree with former Defense Secretary Robert McNamara's observations in his book[9] where he described his thinking during that time in our nation's history that some call "McNamara's War," regardless of whether you served or chose not to serve if you were of an age to do so, and regardless of whether you (as is the case of all the twenty-somethings or even thirty-something around us) were too young to remember it personally and know of it only by listening to those older folk talk about it or by what you read in magazines or history books, the truth is...the Vietnam War is STILL affecting us.
The families and loved ones of slain soldiers are still affected, the careers and reputations of those who "dodged" the draft are still being affected, the wounded are still affected, those who returned to less-than-congratulatory receptions even though they laid their lives on the line for us are still greatly affected, and our nation's policies concerning future conflicts have been greatly affected.

But some "lingering effects" don't need to linger any longer.

The time has come to "put away" grudges against those who didn't share our particular views on the subject, toward those who made decisions on our behalf that we might have disagreed with, etc. It's time for HEALING and RECONCILIATION.

We can learn from the difficult lessons of Vietnam, but there's no need to keep fighting the war in our minds. We need to join hands and, together, face the future—learning from the past, but deliberately choosing to not constantly dwell on it.

The same is true concerning a Christian's past sins.

It is true that some consequences of sin are inevitable, unavoidable, and damaging: broken relationships, legal or punitive consequences, the physical consequences of abuse, etc., are going to occur whether we're a believer or not a believer.

But some consequences only remain if we choose to let them continue, choosing to keep them active, cultivating them unnecessarily. These are things we need to let go of.

To the reader...

Today I appeal to you...it's time to allow God's forgiveness and pardon to be a reality in your heart and life.

If you confess your sin to God, and turn to Him as Lord, leader of your life from this point forward, He will forgive you...forever.

If you're a believer and have already experienced His forgiveness, then I urge you to let Him empower you today to FORGIVE YOURSELF. And, if someone has hurt you, offended you, etc., today is the time to let go of it...turning it over to the Lord and letting the "war" stop in your own heart.

Will you let Him bring you peace?

Will you be free from the burden of sin? There's power in the blood of the Lamb of God, which was spilled for you on the battlefield of a cross on a hill.

He took the hill...He won the battle...He's offering you a fresh start.

To the Lord…

Thank You for wiping away the penalty of my sin.

Help me, Lord, to never again be victim of self-inflicting wounds…of sin, and of holding on to that which You've already taken from me…guilt.

Help me instead to focus on the new, the fresh, the bright future You have for me.

THE GOLDEN CALF...Uhh, PARLOR

Years ago a certain evangelical pastor in a very "fashion-conscious" city church started a work among teenage guys from the slums. He played basketball with them, talked to them on their "turf," and managed to bring many of them into the church's parlor for various meetings, Bible studies, etc. He taught them the way of salvation, and several of the young men came to receive Jesus as personal Lord and Savior.

The pastor was excited to see how God was working...

But some of the church's members were NOT so happy about it all.

Grumblings began among the church people, centering around how the pastor was changing their "image" in the community. Whereas all the rest of the church leaders and former leaders, former pastors, and all the current long-standing members of the church had ALWAYS been aware of and were careful to maintain their "glorious" and spotless reputation for being folks of aristocratic refinery, this pastor was now allowing those slum boys to (O my, perish the thought!) possibly soil the carpets and upholstery, even risking possibly soiling or scratching the lovely gold-plated fixtures in the church's parlor. Egad! Aghast! Alas!

What on earth was the matter with him?!

Didn't he know that Mrs. Flossie had donated that furniture from Paris, and that Mr. and Mrs. Frumpfixel had donated the lovely oil painting of their mother all the way from India. Was he not aware that only folks above the age of respectability (at least in their fifties, mind you) had ever before been allowed any regular meeting time in that sacred of all sacred cows?

Apparently, he must either not be aware or he doesn't really care.

So...the pastor was called before the church to give an account of the "damage" he was doing, and explain what his intentions were, what he planned to do bout about the slum boys "invading" the parlor.

His defense went like this:

"Brethren, when called to give an account to my Master, what shall I say? 'Here, Lord, is the church You entrusted to me. It is in good shape. Passersby are oft heard to mention how refined and closely-guarded our traditions of exclusivity and elitism are, actions which have allowed us to maintain an intimate and familiar membership over the years. And...the ornate, golden church parlor is especially impeccable. The carpets and upholsteries are good as new, all nice and clean!'? If so, might He not say to me in return, 'Where are the SOULS which I sent you to win for Me? Where are the boys?'"

To the reader...

Are there some golden calves, some "sacred cows" in your life?

Are you mindful that everything you "possess" you really don't possess at all, that it has been merely "loaned" to you by God to use during your sojourn on earth? Are you aware that there will come a day when you'll pass from this earth and someone else will "possess" those things?

And, more importantly, are you aware that God is much more interested in what you DO than what you HAVE?

I encourage you today...use what God has given you to influence the lives of others...to point them toward their need for a relationship with Jesus.

And then...get out of the parlor and go play some basketball with the kids in the neighborhood...it's time far better spent.

By the way, teenagers, go for it! I'm looking forward to seeing how God grows you into the person He created you to be for His glory.

To the Lord...

Thank You that You have allowed me to part of a church where souls are more important than history, and where young people—even with their sometimes spills and still-developing maturity—are not merely looked upon as the church of tomorrow, but they are the church today, and the leaders of the church tomorrow.

Thank You that if they give You a chance You will shine in them and out of them to others.

THE CASE OF THE CUSTOM-MADE EAR PLUGS

The Pentagon has just ordered custom-made ear plugs for some of our troops…at the tune of $65 per set!

The "powers that be" have decided that one particular group of soldiers is suffering the possibility of dramatic and life-time hearing loss by being dangerously placed in "a noise-hazard environment" and need some relief in order to not suffering a hearing loss.

Okay, that seems logical enough, right? After all, with all that artillery fire going on, all those loud rounds on the battlefield, etc., it's only to be expected, don't you think?

Well, that would be true, except these ear plugs are NOT for the ground troops, NOT for the soldiers in the trenches, NOT for those in the heat of the battle…

These ear plugs are for the military BAND members!

And where is this "noise-hazard environment," you ask? Well, the musicians are being (and I quote) "imperiled…because many of their practice sessions take place not on fresh-air parade grounds but indoors, where the massed sound of brass and snare constitutes….a noise-hazard environment!"

Now, please don't take me wrong…I'm a fan of military bands. I'm a fan of bands in general. In fact, in addition to playing in school marching bands and concert bands from the time I was in the fifth grade through my early college years, I also played a couple of concerts along with the National Guard Armory Band in Springfield, Missouri, while I was a high school senior. They needed a tuba player to "round out" their sound and I gladly rehearsed in their gym and played in their concerts...one of many band concerts. Believe me, I know how "loud" it can get during rehearsals indoors. However, purchasing ear plugs is an example of the mistake of...

Treating the symptom instead of the problem.

The problem is where they're practicing! The solution is to either practice in larger rooms, build more acoustic rehearsal areas (cheaper in the long run than issuing custom-made ear plugs for years to come), or to simply move outdoors...where the rest of the troops do THEIR work.

The same principle applies in dealing with spiritual "warfare."

Whereas many try to simply put a "BAND-aid" on problems, trying to change things externally, merely treating symptoms rather than the real problem. God says the solution to spiritual matters can only be found in repentance and turn to Him. He then cures what's wrong by changing our location...moving us from being caught up in the thinking and attempted solutions of the world, and moving to relying on God's power alone.

To the reader...
    I hope you'll come out from that small little "rehearsal hall" you're trying to live your life in, and come out to the Light...accepting God's cure for the problem.

To the Lord...
    Thanks for not providing a BAND-aid where only a blood transfusion of Your blood could "cure" my sinful condition.

COMMENCEMENT

Commencement—perhaps one of the most misunderstood words in our culture.

In the weeks ahead colleges, universities, high school after high school and junior high / middle schools too will host "commencement" exercises. However, very few people understand the truth…

There is a big difference between Graduation and Commencement.

I realize many, probably most, who will attend these fetes will not make a distinction. Some will talk about going to graduation and others will call it commencement, and much of the terminology they will use will expose their idea of what the ceremony is all about. Let me explain…

"Graduation" is FROM.

You graduate FROM an institution, you have achieved a certain level of achievement, "mastered" an acceptable percentage of required learnable facts and/or skills, enough to receive a diploma which states you have indeed COMPLETED a prescribed set of courses.

Graduation is an end. You have completed the task, finished the race, and your prize is to dress up as a penguin, walk across a stage, receive a sheepskin with scribbling on it, and listen to your family and friends howl like ravenous wolves in the audience (even though they were instructed by you and the school administration to not do such things).

It's over. It's done. You'll say good bye to many you've developed a relationship over the years, and whether you realize it or not, after today you will literally never see many of them again for the rest of your life.

It is a "pausable moment," a Kodak moment that you have EARNED, and one for which we rightfully and proudly recognize you for having accomplished.

However, while graduation is from, Commencement is TO.

Commencement does not mean an end, but a BEGINNING.
When you commence something, you are beginning it. In this case you are commencing the rest of your life, now "equipped" with a level of education that many, and most in some parts of the word, will never achieve.

High school and college grads, you are to be congratulated for "sticking it out" and finishing, but in the weeks to come, grads, I encourage you to remember these things:

a) A high school or college or graduate level education is only a benefit to you if you choose to CONTINUE to learn. In Ozarkian lingo it means, "If you don't ever stop learning, NOW you're truly educated." The ultimate goal of education is to teach you how to teach yourself throughout the rest of your life, to continue to learn.

b) You didn't reach this level of education by yourself. You had the help of teachers, writers of textbooks, other students, principals and administrators...AND your family. Don't forget these people after you receive your diploma. Don't exclude these people from your celebrations. In a very real sense, THEY are "graduating" too, and they will also be invisible helpers in your "commencement" to future learning and maturity.

c) Many who have NOT received the formal training you have received still know more about life than you do. Don't be a snob. Don't "look down on" grandma or grandpa or mom or dad. They've learned a lot about life that was never taught in any of your textbooks, things you still have ahead of you to learn. These people are not your enemies, they're on your side. Be wise. "Tap" their knowledge. Listen to their advice. Life IS like a box of chocolates...because it's made to be SHARED with others.

d) And finally, don't forget where ALL truth really dwells. Jesus made an outrageous claim, but a factual one, when He said, "I AM the truth." As you commence the rest of your life you'll receive lots of "words of wisdom" from lots of sources...some with even bigger diplomas than yours, folk who even teach at institutions of higher learning...but remember: there's only ONE source of REAL TRUTH—JESUS!

To the reader...

    I invite you to show some real "class" in how you commence with the rest of your life...starting today.

To the Lord...

    Thank You for allowing me to graduate FROM being lost in my sin TO being saved by Your grace.

    Now, Lord, I ask your help as I commence the rest of my life.

    I am fully aware that whatever awards or accolades I receive are actually Yours, as You are the source of all good things, and my motivation for seeking to achieve, so that I might bring honor to You.

RIGHT MOTIVE, WRONG METHOD

Monday night's event was designed and intended to help deal with a community problem, to be an encouragement, in short…to make a difference!

There motives were right, but their method was wrong.

Two North Carolina minor league baseball teams, the Winston-Salem Warthogs (great name, huh?) and the Durham Bulls managed to complete a whole 2 and 2/3 innings of their game in about 25 minutes.[10] Within that time, four different batters had been hit by pitches from the opposing pitchers. The last of the victims, Durham's John Krott, was hit by a pitch from Warthog Jason Kummerfeldt, and then charged the mound, setting off a brawl that emptied both benches, lasted 32 minutes, and resulted in a total of ten players being ejected from the game. One of them, Glen Cullop, suffered the loss of several of his teeth and was knocked unconscious. He underwent surgery on Wednesday and remained hospitalized until Friday afternoon.

All of those ejected face a minimum two game suspension and a $100 fine, but the irony of all of this is…

All of this happened on "Strike Out Domestic Violence Night!"

As admirable as the promoters' motive was in desiring to help bring an end to domestic violence, there's a real simple answer to why the promoters were disappointed, why the players "blew it," and why many of the fans ended up being so disgusted that they even demanded their money back…

You don't cure cancer with band-aids.

Watching eighteen guys in jumpsuits throw balls and swing bats is NOT going to make one iota's difference in the INSIDE problem of domestic violence.

In the same way, condoms are a similarly flawed "band-aid" approach being presented as a "cure" for the teenage pregnancy epidemic and the spread of the A.I.D.S. virus, the "just say no" campaign, as admirable an attempt as it might be, will never succeed in wiping out drug addiction, and America will never return to being a moral and God-fearing nation again by simply singing songs and waving flags.

Instead of merely hosting a baseball game, it's a shame the promoters didn't put the emphasis on where the cure is...presenting Jesus to all who were present—and especially to those swinging bats and throwing balls and punches at one another.

You see, it's impossible to truly "say no" until you "say YES" to Jesus, because He alone brings the change of heart that is the real cure for what is wrong on the inside of person's hearts that leads them to be violent toward their mates, their children, even violent towards themselves.

To the reader...

Are you ready to turn from "band-aids" to the real cure to the personal turmoil in your life? Are you ready to end the "game" and begin truly living?

Come on...round third and "come safely home" to Jesus.

To the Lord...

It wasn't three strikes, but thirty-nine stripes You took for me, Lord.

Thank You for experiencing the violence in my place, then giving me Your peace.

REAL MEN GROW UP

Are you ready for a startling truth? Here goes… "Mothers give birth to children."

Pretty profound, huh? Earth-shaking in its implications, isn't it?

Well, let me word it another way…

No one is born a man.

We do not inherit maturity. You don't become a real man overnight, nor is one a real man merely because he can jump higher, run faster, or shoot straighter than when he was a boy. Not even the siring of children makes one a man, because being a real man is not connected merely to any physical attributes…it is more than just being male.

Moms give birth to boys. Whether or not these boys ever become men depends upon their willingness to mature each day, and accept the responsibilities that come with being a real man.

Consequently…

There are 75-year old boys and 17-year old men in this world.

Part of what it takes to become a real man is realizing that God made us male and it is He and He alone who provides us the experiences, the preparation we need to mature us into the men He desires us to be. He prepares us for the big challenges and blessings along the journey. If we will accept His gifts, learn His secrets, and allow Him to grow us, the day will come when we will indeed be the real men He created us to be, and when we will indeed…

OBSERVATIONS FROM THE WEIRD BEARDED GUY

"Rise up, O men of God; be done with lesser things."[11]

I'm reminded of the story of the man stranded in the desert, thirsty, desperate for water. Amazingly enough he came upon another man, well-clad and calm. The thirsty wanderer asked the well-clad man for a drink of water, to which the well-clad man responded, "Oh, I don't have water here, but I can give you this shirt."

"No," the wonderer said, "I don't need a shirt, I need water."

And, with this, he staggered on, looking again for something to drink. After awhile, now much thirstier, he came upon a second well-clad man, to which the wanderer made the request again, "Please, sir, may I have some water?"

The well-clad man answered him, saying, "Oh, I don't have water here, my friend, but I can give you this necktie."

"No," the wanderer said, "I don't need a necktie; I need water."

And once again he staggered on, desperately seeking what he craved the most: water to quench his thirst. After he thought he could go no further, he suddenly came upon—amazing as it might seem—a restaurant in the middle of the desert! What a relief! What a great discovery, the wanderer thought!

So, approaching the cafe with renewed energy, he came to the front door and spoke to the maitre-d, saying, "Oh, how wonderful it is to see you here, sir. Please let me come in and drink some water."

However, the maitre-d responded, saying, "I'm sorry, sir, but a shirt and a tie are required to come in here."

> Men, we too must allow God to prepare us for what
> He has in mind later on.

We're not born men, we mature into them by accepting the events and provisions of God along the way that bring us to the "restaurant in the desert" fully prepared to enjoy the feast God has in mind for us.

To the reader...

How about it, mister? Are you trusting God in the every day stuff? Are you letting Him lead you to tomorrow?

It's the way to manhood.

And, ladies, it's also the way God will mature you as a woman to meet the challenges and reap the rewards of maturity.

Are you trusting God to lead you there?

To the Lord…

Help me, as a man, to depend on You.

And help me as a disciple to continue bringing Living Water to a dry and thirsty land, to wanderers You bring across my path.

LOST, FOUND, REJOICING

Six days earlier, "protected" inside a U. S. F-16 fighter jet, Captain Scott O'Grady learned up-close and personally the nightmare of all pilots: he was shot down over enemy territory.

Scott was literally LOST.

Neither he nor the rest of the world knew his whereabouts other than the fact he was in enemy territory, and while he stayed hidden from the troops of Bosnia, the world waited to see if he was still among the living. While Scott sent signals from a running-low battery, military officials tried to decipher if these signals were a decoy from the enemy or from Scott himself. Scott ate the last of his survival kit food, slept under heavy brush, and finally managed to survive by eating bugs and drinking rain water.

Then came word.

Not only were the signals really from Scott, but a rescue attempt under cover of dawn by four helicopters and twenty specially-trained Marines facing surface-to-air missile attacks and small arms fire successfully rescued Scott, returning him to his "home" base.

Within minutes, his dad on the East coast, mom on the West coast, then from the President on down through the National Security Secretary, Pentagon officials…all the way to and through the ranks of the rescue team, and, of course, Scott too, all did the same thing…they rejoiced![12] Rightly so.

But, believe it or not, a similar experience happened in MY life.

No, I've never been to Bosnia, never been in an F-16, and I've never resorted to eating bugs and rain water in order to survive, but nonetheless I was indeed LOST, then RESCUED, and there was much REJOICING.

As a nine-year old boy I came to realize I was LOST…in sin.

I realized too that I was actually in the enemy camp…having rejected Jesus.

But when I finally responded to the Lord, He RESCUED me…saved me from the penalty my sin had caused: separation from Him.

And immediately there was much REJOICING…in heaven! (see Luke 15:7), on earth (in my family), and in my heart (there's no greater rejoicing than to know you've been forgiven, adopted into God's family, washed clean of sin, and given a brand new life—a life abundant and forever!).

To the reader…

If you've never been saved, rescued from the penalty of your sin, why not respond to Jesus' sacrificial signal—He gave His life for you—and let Him bring you home?

Heaven and earth are waiting to rejoice with you.

To the Lord…

Thanks for sending the rain of Your shed blood that rescued me from spiritual captivity.

And, by the way, thanks too that no bugs were involved in my rescue.

WHAT'S RIGHT WITH AMERICA

Sometimes the court cases seem to drag on forever. Sometimes a guilty felon is released on a technicality because his or her rights were inadvertently violated somewhere in the process of judgment. And sometimes the jury gets it wrong.

Sometimes a business doesn't make it and has to close its doors. Can you say "Enron" or T.W.A.?

Sometimes the line at the Social Security Office will mean an hour's wait in order to receive disability payments. (And usually, even though there are twenty five windows to serve the crowd, only one will be open at a time.)

Sometimes the line is even longer waiting at a voting booth, and even afterwards it can take weeks for a final decision to come down as to who was elected President while election "experts" look at the "hanging chads" of some ballots that were cast.

But all of these are part of what makes America a great country.

Lengthy court cases can indeed be irritating sometimes. I never thought O.J.'s trial or the farce of the court case involving Anna Nicole Smith would ever end, but then I had to remind myself…lengthy court cases are NOT a part of life in many countries in the world…because they don't grant people the "right" to a fair trial by a jury of their peers.
Instead, those who are accused of a crime are sentenced by something akin to a kangaroo court or languish in jails for years without ever even having a hearing, so the fact that back here in the States an occasional felon "escapes" on a technicality is actually a small price to pay for having the right to be presumed innocent until proven guilty and the right to protection from unreasonable search and seizure, etc.

For a business to close its doors meant it at least had the chance to OPEN in the first place. In some socialist societies citizens can't own a business. In fact all the property in the state belongs to the state, OR the state receives any profits from the business beyond a paltry stipend for covering expenses.

Lines at the Social Security Administration Office might be irritating in the short run, but the very existence of the Social Security Administration says a lot about a nation who wants to take care of its elderly citizens and those in need.

Yet, of all the above "problems" the greatest, I think, is long lines at voting booths. As United States citizens we have both the right and the responsibility to cast a vote in determining the direction our country goes. That is a privilege folk in many countries can only dream about.

So, sure, there are a lot of things about America that need improving, but there are also lots of things RIGHT with America.

America—Love it…and help revive it!

To the reader…

I encourage you to not wait for a holiday to come along to stop and be thankful the Lord has allowed you to live in America. It's not a perfect country, but it's certainly far ahead of any of the rest!

To the Lord…

Thank You for the freedom You have brought into my life…not just the governmental freedom we enjoy in America, but for having set me free from the bondage of sin, free to enjoy life, and the assurance of life eternal with You.

THE DISGUISE OF ACTIVITY

Dr. James A. Pike died in 1969. His life COULD be described as one of constant change and upheaval. Of course, that would be saying it politely, and it would not give a full account of what really happened, or, as Paul Harvey would describe it, it would be leaving out the meat because it wouldn't be telling "the rest of the story."

The brutal truth is this: the Right Reverend James A. Pike, priest, bishop, writer, and hypocrite of the first order, died amid religious activity disguised as genuine faith.

There, that says it more accurately.

During his lifetime, Dr. Pike turned from the practice of law to the priesthood within the Catholic Church. He eventually became a bishop, but then converted from Catholicism to become a Protestant minister. He also went from being an alcoholic and chain-smoker to practicing total abstinence.

And yet, his life was one of upheaval because in the midst of all the religious "trappings" lived a man who never truly gave his heart over to the Lord. He never made a public declaration of a changed life brought about through a commitment to and a reliance upon Jesus as personal Savior and Lord. In fact, he scoffed at such an idea.

The lesson to be learned from Pike?...

Activity is no substitute for faith.

If you only looked at the external, you might believe Pike was a believer. After all, there was a lot of "religious activity" in his life. But a lack of faith is often disguised by activity. He looks busy, so he must be sincere, right? No. Sometimes he's busy because he's terribly confused or misguided.

OBSERVATIONS FROM THE WEIRD BEARDED GUY

Ironically, James Pike died while he was researching a new book on the historicity of Jesus. Wishing to rummage through old bookstalls in Jerusalem and to walk where Jesus walked, Dr. and Mrs. Pike had gone to the Holy Land in search of information and inspiration. Dr. Pike was a doubter who desperately sought something he hoped would prove to be "concrete" to rest his faith upon. Scripture tells us that faith IS that substance, that assurance of what is unseen, what is hoped for, and the solidity, the reliability of our faith is found in the reality that Jesus is Who He says He is, and the Bible has accurately recorded what He did, flowing out of Who He is.

But, as I said earlier, Pike was not a man of faith, he was merely a man of activity.

So, while driving through one of the deserts in the Holy Land on a hot August afternoon, Dr. Pike and his wife became lost. Following a series of grueling experiences, Mrs. Pike finally secured help, but it was TOO LATE.

Her fifty-six year old husband was dead.

A writer for Time magazine reported on the irony of the fact that the Right Reverend James A. Pike, once again on the brink of something new, "should perish in the wilderness of the Judean desert, looking for Jesus."[13]

A friend of mine, reacting to the story commented, "Yes, and to think he could have found Jesus in California!"

To the reader…

Let me ask you a couple of questions:

a) Are you looking for Jesus in some "remote" place? Are you perhaps waiting for some "bizarre" occurrence to "get your attention?"— He's here, and He's ready to meet you now…right where You are.

b) Are you "busy" getting to KNOW Him and to OBEY Him, or are you just "busy?" I pray you'll understand and see the truth as it is: Yes, real faith is active, but not all activity is based on real faith. Sometimes activity is merely trying to disguise itself as faith.

To the Lord…

Please help me remember today that Your real business is NOT "busy-ness."

DOING "THE WAVE"

We've all seen it…a crowd at a sporting event synchronizes rising from their seats with their hands in the air to simulate a giant ocean wave. It's pretty cool…although I must say it's a pet peeve of mine for fans to be focused on doing "the wave" at times in the middle of a game when their team needs their attention and encouragement instead of their self-fascination with creating imaginary imaging of ocean movements.

But, actually, it's not that kind of wave I want to talk about here at all.

I want to tell you about how two boys affected their world by simply waving at it.

We can learn something today from Caleb Miller, age eleven, the grandson of my friend and counseling colleague Ann Miller, and Brian Stoddard, age eight, Caleb's friend and co-conspirator in "the wave experiment."

These two young men decided that since they didn't have anything else to do in their small town (Lima, Ohio—population 55,000) (their soccer game had been cancelled and they didn't feel like going to the swimming pool), they would see if they could get 500 people to save back at them if they waved first.

So, they "got all dressed up in some nice jeans and a good-looking t-shirt" (Caleb's words), and stood on one of the street corners in Lima, where they started waving to passersby. They considered each car as only one person—even if it was a van with ten people in it waving back at them.

At four o'clock, two hours into their "mission," they had already passed their goal of 500, so they decided to UP the goal to 1,000 by supper time.

Things went along smoothly until it started to rain and the wind started blowing. Still Caleb and Brian stayed at their posts. They were closing in on 1,000 when lightning started to hit, and they finally had to call it quits for safety's sake.

But that wasn't the end of the story at all.

One lady in town was so "touched" by their act of innocent kindness, she went and told their story to the local newspaper, who reported the boys' feat on the front page of the Lima News. Soon a television station picked up the story also.

However, the crowning acclaim came just two days later, on Caleb's eleventh birthday, when The Tonight Show called and asked the two boys to come and appear on its Wednesday program.

Caleb and Brian flew to Los Angeles FREE, stayed in the Beverly Hilton FREE, and appeared on national television...simply because they waved to people and wouldn't stop waving until they had "reached out and touched" 1,000 lives.

Way to go, Caleb and Brian! You're an inspiration to us all.

To the reader...
This week, let's consider beginning our own "wave ministry" by looking for opportunities to smile, wave, and speak a word of cheer, a word of encouragement.

No, we'll not end up on national television for it...that's already been done, but let's do it anyway. Everyone can use the encouragement.

To the Lord...
Thanks, Lord, for reaching out and touching my life with Your love.

ANIMALS GONE WILD!

In the past two months across America a strange phenomenon has been taking place...

It seems the animals have gone wild!

In New York City four pigs were caught wandering loose, while in Minneapolis a circus kangaroo broke free from the confines of his (or her?) circus train car and went sight-seeing. Folks traveling via the Kansas City International Airport saw what some might have thought was an exhibit from the Bass Pro Shops headquarters 150 miles south in Springfield, but it was a live deer frolicking loose down the terminal halls. All the while, residents in a Hollidaysburg, Pennsylvania, neighborhood worked together to try and capture a monkey roaming the back alleys and hanging on fences and trees. Then, although nothing earth-shaking is supposed to happen in Toledo, Ohio, the ground DID shake in June when two elephants walked out their cage in the Toledo Zoo and strolled around the park (no telling how many folk fed them peanuts really close-up), but my FAVORITE one of these disturbing encounters of all happened in Cincinnati, where...

A goose snatched a golfer's 2-iron at the Pebble Creek Golf Course, then ran off with it!

Imagine! (As though anyone can successfully hit a 2-iron anyway!) I didn't ever learn the final results, but I would have loved to have seen the golfers on the course chasing after the goose. I mean, I've watched a lot of fellows and gals trying to "get a birdie" on the course before, but this is ridiculous! Plus, this time the birdie got them!

OBSERVATIONS FROM THE WEIRD BEARDED GUY

Well, you say, it's all amusing, but I'm not going to encounter any loose animals today, so why are you bothering to tell me about these things?

I wouldn't be too sure of that if I were you...I think if you look around you'll probably discover that God is going to bring across your path today a lot of people who have gone wild. They may have, at one time, been in control, where they belonged, doing what they should have been, but something has happened...now they're struggling, they're aware that they're lost, and they're in need of some help.

In fact, Jesus even described the whole human race as being like sheep without a shepherd, and explained that He had come to seek and save those who are lost. He even told how He, the Good Shepherd, is not content to remain with the ninety-nine sheep who are into the fold when there is still one lost sheep that needs to be found.

To the reader...

Do you feel like your life is out of control, that you're lost and need to come home? Well, Jesus is the way home to the Father.

He's the Good Shepherd Who has laid His life down for the sheep.

He's the Great Physician Who can mend broken hearts.

Today, in the middle of your situation, whatever it might be, rest assured of this,

He knows where you are, and He has the power to "make it right" again.

All-ee All-ee in free! Let the hiding be over, Jesus is seeking you.

To the Lord...

Thanks for bringing me home and watching over me as my loving shepherd.

And thanks for not just showing the way, but BEING the way home.

THE CARPENTER DOES BATHROOMS TOO

The smell of fresh paint is still strong inside the parsonage today.
While Kim and Jeff were with other teenagers at the summer Youth Camp in New Mexico, Becky and I decided to paint the front restroom in the parsonage...

And I saw some spiritual lessons in the middle of it.

The condition of the walls before painting was pretty desperate: a lack of ventilation had led to some mildewing, moisture / vapors had led to a great deal of unsightly peeling, and some caulking and sealing was needed around the edge of the tub. All in all, it was clearly more than a one day job. So, we made the necessary preparations, scheduled the project while the restroom would be free of traffic for a few days, and set out to fix what needed to be fixed.

Here's spiritual application #1:
Maybe today you feel like your life is at the point of desperation, needing to be fixed and "sealed." If so, it's time to call on the Master Carpenter, Jesus, to do the work for you and in you.

Back to the work...first came the preparations. Before anything could be done, supplies (paint, brushes, roller, roller pan, spackling powder, masking tape, sand paper, putty knife, drop cloth) had to be selected and purchased, the cloth had to be put in place, and our old clothes had to be put on. The walls then needed to be bleached, scraped, spackled and sanded.

Becky bleached, did a preliminary "scrape" of the ceiling, caulked the gaps in the tub, and we put the drop cloth down. Then I did a "final" scraping, spackled, sanded, masked, prepared the brushes and roller, and opened and stirred the paint.

Here's spiritual application #2:
Many Christians play the role of being the "preparers" of hearts. Maybe they're not the ones who actually "apply the paint" when it comes to leading folk to a saving relationship with Jesus, but they play a much-needed role by helping prepare the way: they lay down the "drop cloth" or foundation of prayer, help sand away and prepare hearts through showing love to folks with "holes" in their lives, and apply the "spackle" of a consistent Godly life, helping "open the bucket" by inviting folk to Bible Study and worship, all very important in the overall process of "painting" new lives.

Back to the work again...before I could apply the heavy paint (using a roller), the walls and ceiling had to be "cut in" around the corners and edges and other tight places with brushes. Then came the "main event" of applying the paint that covered the "old coat" along with all the spackle stains and the "filled holes."

The old walls received gladly the fresh coat of paint (in this case it took two coats, but the spiritual application still applies) and the result...it looked, even smelled...brand new!

Here's spiritual application #3:
Although people can help out in preparing your heart, praying for you, telling you of the wonderful life the Lord has in store for you, etc, and although the Holy Spirit can "cut in" and make everything ready and possible for the final coat, you have to choose to receive the blood of Jesus to "cover" the penalty of your sin, to "fill" the vacuum in hour heart which only He can fill, and to allow you to become NEW, born again, and fresh as a new-born, with the "aroma" of the Holy Spirit permeating your existence and bringing the fruit of the Spirit.

By the way, in contrast to my bathroom, one coat is all you'll ever need once the "enamel" of Jesus' blood is applied to your sinful, crimson heart.

To the reader…

How about you? Are you ready for a new, re-modeled you?

Are you ready to let Jesus re-create you, to make you new, clean, fresh, joyful?

Then let the paint roll!

To the Lord…

Thank You for all the sanding, bleaching, scraping and spackling You have brought into my life, preparing me to become the person You have in mind for me to be.

Thank You most of all, though, for the blood You applied to my stained and "mildewed" life…one coat has covered me for all of eternity!

CHEER UP!

It's official: the hazy, crazy days of summer have made their way through the hourglass and the sands of time, and have brought us that often-feared, often-loathed, but much-anticipated time of the year…it's time to go BACK TO SCHOOL!

So, to all the students and parents of students who might read this, let me say…

Cheer up!

The truth is, I don't remember too many of the "official" cheers from my school days (mostly I think that's because I was paying more attention to the cheerleaders themselves that any cheers they might be leading), but I do remember one cheer, and it has an appropriate application for this time of the year.

The cheer itself went like this…

LEAN TO THE LEFT!—And, of course, the entire rooting section would bend from the waist and lean as far to the left as they possibly could.

LEAN TO THE RIGHT!—Likewise, the section would lean to the right this time.

STAND UP!—Everyone would then jump up high into the air.

SIT DOWN!—This one is pretty easy to figure out what they did.

FIGHT! FIGHT! FIGHT!—The crowd would shout these words as loud as possible with fists clenched and arms moving like a baseball pitcher throwing a ball in time with each "fight" word shouted.

There was certainly nothing truly profound in what was said, but it actually IS the basis for my "cheer" to students and their parents today as you face the new school year, because...

Every part of the cheer will be represented in your school this year.

First, there's the FIGHT GROUP.
There are some who will spend their whole school year "fighting" authority.

They'll try to see how for they can go in defying the teachers, professors, principals, their parents, the police, their Bible Study leaders, youth leaders, and spiritual leaders God has put in their lives.

The consequence of their actions will be that they'll spend their entire year LOSING. You see, no team can win when it concentrates its efforts in fighting someone or something OTHER than their opponent.

If you find yourself identifying with this group, cheer up! Realize that your teachers, administrators, parents, authority figures in general, are not your enemy. They are actually on your side, and they want to help you. So let them. Follow their leadership and you'll avoid a whole lot of unnecessary grief this year.

Then there will be those who LEAN TO THE LEFT, LEAN TO THE RIGHT.

It's amazing to me how many teenagers and college students SAY they want to be "unique," "their own person," and don't want to be told what to do by anyone, but they don't really mean it. How do I know? Because they'll end up wearing exactly the same clothes as the rest of the crowd, cut their hair the same, use the same lingo, listen to the same music, go to the same places, and do the same things as the "herd."

In essence they're giving away their little "secret"—they don't really have the courage yet to be unique at all. They just want to "blend in" and follow the crowd.

If this is where you find yourself, my encouragement to you is to practice instead the last two parts of the cheer...

The STAND UP Group!

There are some reading this who have NOT bought in to the idea that conformity is the route to being unique.

To you I say, congratulations, mature ones!

To the rest I say, this year take a stand for the Lord.

Yes, it will be tough at first, because you'll be swimming against the current, but you can do it with the Lord's help, and you'll receive the MOST help from Him when you become a part of…

The SIT DOWN Group.

I invite you to join this "elite of the elite" group who has learned to sit down every morning and study His Word, and also sit down every Sunday and during the week and listen to His truths being preached and taught at church.

I invite you to sit down and give an open ear's listen to those the Lord has put in spiritual authority over you.

When you do, I promise you, you'll be on the WINNING TEAM this season!

SO…Give me a J! Give me an E! Give me an S! Give me a U! Give me another S!
What's that spell?…VICTORY, because victory is only found in Jesus.

To the reader…

Cheer up! Jesus is ready to lead you to victory if you'll put your faith and trust in Him as Lord of your life.

To the Lord…

Thank You that You did the fighting for me, and won the victory for my soul.

Thank You for leading me to victory after victory in my own life as I've trusted Your leadership and followed Your instructions.

Thank You for giving me the courage to stand up.

And thank You for all You teach me when I sit down and listen to Your Word.

You're Number One, Jesus!

LOVE BRACELETS

When Victoria Ingram and Randall Curlee got married last year, the chapel was adorned with flowers, their family and friends were present, the bride wore her engagement ring, and both the bride AND the groom wore bracelets...

Hospital bracelets.

Traditional vows were exchanged, but when the minister talked about the importance of giving of ourselves in order for a relationship to be all it can be, the bride smiled, and the groom could no longer hold back his tears. You see, Victoria and Randall's wedding took place in the chapel of the hospital where they were about to go into surgery...together.
Kind of a strange honeymoon, huh?
They were married while still in the hospital so Victoria could give Randall a kidney that could save his life. Victoria, 45, said she was doing nothing more than anyone would. "If anyone was in need," she concluded, "wouldn't you give YOUR kidney? He's my pal, and it's our life."[15]
In offering a kidney, Victoria was saving her husband-to-be from blindness, damage to his heart and blood vessels, and circulatory problems in his legs. She was, of course, also risking complications in her own body that surgery can sometimes bring, but...

She loves Randall, and she felt her "gift" was well worth it.

Wow! That is true love, huh?

OBSERVATIONS FROM THE WEIRD BEARDED GUY

But you know what? Jesus gave you even MORE!

You see, He gave His very LIFE. And, in return, He provided more than life for you and me... He gave us life abundant and eternal also.

We can't earn it, nor will we ever deserve it, He simply gave it to us.

You see, Jesus truly loves you, and He has gone beyond just telling you so, He's proven it to be so by dying in your place on the cross.

To those who have received Him, He has saved us from spiritual blindness.

He has saved us from damage to our hearts because He keeps us from being cold-hearted by giving us a love for others that can never be experienced in any other way.

He has even given our legs a new mission: to go and carry His message to others.

To the reader...

As you reflect on His great gift, let me ask you a couple of questions today:

a) Have you already received the gift of everlasting and abundant life that Jesus gave His life in order to give to you? If not, why not do so right now?

b) If you have received Him, are your willing to give to others? You see, giving IS important in relationships because giving it is ESSENCE of love. Victoria and Randall know that, and Jesus explained it this way, "For God so loved the world, that He GAVE His only Son..."

To the Lord...

Thank You that Your "I. D. Bracelet" had my name on it... You took my place on the cross and gave Your life for mine.

PRECIOUS MEMORIES

(Note: This article was written twelve years ago, but it's still as fresh on my heart as if the events just occurred yesterday...)

"Precious memories, how they linger."[16]
Those lyrics are certainly true today as this is a weekend full of special memories...

Yesterday marked the fiftieth anniversary of VJ Day (Victory over Japan), when Emperor Hirohito signed the official surrender of the Japanese forces to the Allies while aboard the USS Missouri, marking the official end of World War II. I wasn't around then, but I've seen the pictures.

Yesterday also marked the opening of the Rock 'n Roll Hall of Fame, remembering the events and persons who brought the idiom of rock 'n roll to the ears (and some would say the ruin) of the world.

Today marks my fourth anniversary as pastor of Bethany Baptist Church, and in looking back I recall so many who have come to faith in Christ, been baptized, have moved their families and have joined their lives with ours in being a part of God's work here. It has been a blessed time in my life and in the life of God's ministry through Bethany, and I look forward to greater and greater service in the years to come.

However, as important as all these memories are, the greatest to me is...

The birth of Kim Gilbert seventeen years ago today.

As Kim brought to Becky's attention and mine this past week (bringing on some choked-up tears), this might be the last birthday Kim celebrates while living in our home. This time next year our "little girl" most likely will be living in a college dormitory.

(Note: Let me insert it here twelve years later, as a proud daddy…Kim did indeed go to stay in the honors dormitory at Arizona State University by virtue of being a National Merit Scholar and receiving a "free ride" regarding her tuition for the full four years, and graduated Summa Cum Laude, the highest scholastic honor possible…certainly taking after her mom when it comes to the "smarts" in the family. She's now an English professor at the University of Oklahoma, is married to a wonderful Christian man, Scott, and is expecting her first child this December.)

So, Kim, I want you to know this truth…EVERY DAY you're alive is a celebration for your daddy. Yes, you might be somewhere else on your coming birthdays, but the PARTY will go on in the Gilbert house as we thank God for bringing you into our lives. And, Jeff, the same is true for you. We love both of you, and we're proud of both of you.

This is a day of memories…but today's events will only be the start of all the NEW MEMORIES we'll think about next year at this time.

To the reader…

Can you remember back to a day when you asked Jesus to become your personal Lord and Savior? If not, why not let today be that day in your life?

To the Lord…

Thank You for remembering me, but also for forgetting my sin…forever!

LOVE IN ACTION

There are many "acceptable" ways of telling someone you love them...flowers, candy, long and juicy love letters, hugs, kisses, phone calls, tender shows of affection, etc.

However, the Bible tells us that love is best told NOT by our words, but by our ACTIONS. In John 15:33, Jesus taught, "Greater love has no one than this, that one lay down his life for his friends."

Genevieve Guzman laid down her life this week...for her kids.

This past Saturday Genevieve was minding her own business, going about her normal routine. As was her Saturday custom, she took her two young sons, Emilio (age ten months) and Jesus Oscar Sanchez (age two and a half) with her to the market. Returning from her errand, now pushing a two-seat stroller fully loaded with her two boys and the groceries she just purchased, she made her way down Broadway Road when a gray Oldsmobile Cutlass suddenly came into and, literally, across their path.

Traveling at a speed estimated to be at least 70 miles per hour in a 20 mile per hour speed zone, the car recklessly careened from one side of the road to the other—and then took "dead aim" at the 29-year old mother and her two helplessly unprotected children.

In her last earthly act, Genevieve assessed the situation and realized there was no way to avoid the collision, but her children could be spared if she was willing to sacrifice herself. Mustering her last ounce of strength, she flung the stroller high into the air and away from the scene, throwing her two boys as far as she could, and literally saved her boys from certain death. However, in doing so she gave up any chance for avoiding being hit by the Cutlass herself. The result was tragic, but a testimony of love in action.

OBSERVATIONS FROM THE WEIRD BEARDED GUY

The Cutlass hit Genevieve and threw her in the air, where she landed 60 feet away from the original point of contact. She was killed instantly, but the motorist never even so much as slowed down to check on her or her two children.

As the Cutlass left the scene, little Jesus Sanchez (who, along with Emilio suffered only minor scrapes and bruises from the incident, although he did go into shock) climbed out of his stroller and rushed to his mother's side. Needless to say, he became hysterical.

The memory of WHAT happened to his mother will always be with him, but as he grows older, I pray he will realize WHY she died...because she loved him and showed it.

You are loved too....Jesus proved His love in the same way.

While you and I were unaware of the dangerous condition we were in as sinners, Jesus knew. He stayed on the cross and died so we could live...forever. His sacrificial death for you and I was just as real and just as dramatic a demonstration of His love for you as Genevieve's act of love for her children, but Jesus came back to life...resurrected from the dead, thus conquering forever the penalty and power of death over us.

To the reader...
    If you haven't already, will you accept Jesus' love for you? Will you receive Him as personal Savior and Lord?
    If you will, today will definitely not be "routine" for you.

To the Lord...
    Thank You for laying down Your life for me. Now it's my turn to give my life for Your service and for Your glory and honor.

WALKS LIKE A DUCK, QUACKS LIKE A TURKEY

The Smothers Brothers, balladeers of humor and satire, once re-wrote some of the lyrics of the western ballad, "The Streets of Laredo,"[17] to the following: "I can see by your outfit that you are a cowboy. You can see by my outfit that I'm a cowboy too. (Duet) We can see by our outfits that we are both cowboys…

If you get an outfit you can be a cowboy too!"[18]

Funny stuff, but I've seen the same kind of attitude exhibited on the golf course, too. While money can buy fancy equipment, but that doesn't necessarily mean a person knows how to use it. The same idea holds true for the ski slopes, for surfers, and for many a well-equipped but untalented "wanna-be" rock 'n roll band.

Perhaps one of the most documented cases of this type of "walks like a duck, but quacks like a turkey" phenomena occurred recently at the U. S. Open Tennis Tournament in Flushing Meadows, New York. Pollsters who greeted the fans as they arrived discovered that of those who were dressed in the latest tennis fashions (by the way, a "total outfit" of shorts, shirt, socks, shoes, cap, sweat bands, lip balm, velcro ball-holding rear belts, etc., could run as much as $700), a "smashing" total of 71% admitted to not even having played tennis themselves in more than a year! Hmmm. I guess we should have expected as much from those who are fans of a game where "love" means nothing.

In contrast, in the case of those who were dressed in "normal" clothes (well, it WAS New York, keep in mind), meaning non-tennis clothes or street clothes, more than 60% of them had played an average of twice every week during the same year's period!

Sadly enough, I've discovered the same can also be true within the church.

Some who carry the most expensive Bible might not know how to use it or, if they do know how, might not have opened it for some time.

Some who know all the "lingo," and can identify the major "players" in the Bible might not actually be "in the game" themselves, but just sitting on the sidelines watching, while at the same time trying to "coach" everyone else, convinced that they know more and can do things better than those actually out there chasing each lob and volley.

Some who might sit in the "best seats" on Sunday never "played the game" even once the preceding week, not even one time engaging in any active confronting of the foe, choosing to stay back on the base line, never rushing the net.

Others are "up" on all the "new stuff," new movements, new books and new "styles" of worship, while some prefer the old styles and old strategies, convinced that the "new-fangled" metal rackets will never replace the tried and true wooden ones of the past. However, many in both of these groups can be so "out of shape" spiritually that they wouldn't even last one set, let alone three or more per match and seven matches through the week in order to make it into the tournament finals.

To the reader...

I pray you will let God stir up in you the real YOU, and that you'll actively serve the Lord, not settling for just looking like a Christian from the outside.

To the Lord...

Help me to always remain an active player, never just an armchair quarterback.

And thank You... Your "love" means everything to me.

VANITY, VANITY

God opened the door for my family to sell one car this week (Kim's Colt—a stick shift) and turn around and buy another (Kim's Datsun—an automatic).

Consequently, I had the joy of spending time at the Department of Motor Vehicles—not a pleasant experience. While there I was reminded of the story of Claire Hurd of Lucuet, New Jersey.

Claire works as a "temp" with temporary employment agencies, so she chose a personalized license plate, known as a vanity plate, with the inscription, "TEMP."

That was not a good idea.

Claire has now received 1,400 parking tickets from three different states!

It turns out that ticket writers sometimes write "Temp" in place of a plate number when they issue a ticket to a car with temporary plates, and all those tickets were then assigned to Claire, the owner of the "Temp" license plate.

Eamon Moynihan, who works in Lucuet's Finance Department, said Claire is not the first person to experience this type of problem. He explained: "If you had vanity plates with the word 'BLANK' you might have problems too, because it's just the way the tickets get written sometimes."

Unfortunately for us, license plates aren't the only area where confusion exists.

The Bible tells us that Satan is the very author of confusion, and he's also referred to as the father of lies. He causes confusion by offering "counterfeit" and temporary "solutions" to problems and by accepting false credit for things he never actually did.

OBSERVATIONS FROM THE WEIRD BEARDED GUY

He has managed to successfully TRICK thousands to "buy in" to the counterfeit teachings within the New Age movement by convincing them that any kind of spiritual experience is okay...that all "spiritual" experiences come from God. This, of course, is just as ludicrous as believing every temporary license plate belongs to Claire Hurd.

2 Corinthians 11 tells us that Satan can even disguised himself as "an angel of light," meaning he can convince folk he is a "good guy," when he's actually the devil.

To the reader...

Today, in standing up for what is true, I submit the following truths to you and hope you will accept them as being faithful to God's Word...

a) God alone is the Author of truth, and Jesus IS the Truth, the Way, and the Life.

b) God loves you and has a beautiful and wonderful plan for your life...to bring you the greatest satisfaction possible.

c) What Satan presents to you as a "treat" always has a TRICK attached to it. He always poisons his "goodies" with that which can harm you.

d) God's Word is just that: it's what God has said to you, what He wants you to know, and is always trustworthy as being truth. So, study it. Devour it. Meditate on it. And apply it to your life. Don't let the lies of a fallen angel, the father of lies, deceive you, no matter how "pleasant" and appealing he might make them seem.

To the Lord...

Thank You that You're not just a "temp," but You are forever the Lord.

And, thank You for the treats You bring...without any tricks attached.

SAME MESSAGE, VERY DIFFERENT CROWDS

This week God opened the door for me to speak to a variety of individuals and groups, allowing me to experience the most blessed privilege afforded a human being, the opportunity to join Him in His ministry to those who are hurting, and to some who are lost, having no direction in their lives because they have never received Jesus, THE Way.

In each case, and with each audience, the person's life needs and living circumstances were quite different. In each case, the site and environment surrounding the encounter was distinctively unique. And in each case God's Spirit took over and led our discussion, pointing people to Him, to His unquenchable love for ALL people, and His amazing grace which is willing to forgive and cleanse any who repent and receive Him as Lord.

And yet, the ultimate summary of our discussions was the same...

Jesus is THE answer for whatever circumstance you're experiencing.

For the transient looking for a place to stay the night, Jesus showed him this week that folk who know Jesus DO CARE about people they've never met before and WILL ASSIST them in any way they can to meet physical and "real" needs in their lives.

For the lady whose husband had treated her badly, God reminded her this week that He will NEVER LEAVE HER, never forsake her, and is willing and capable to meet her needs and empower her to face an uncertain future.

For the three men on the golf course scoffing at the "crazy notion" that there is a God to Whom we will all someday bow and give homage, God placed a Baptist preacher in their foursome and began revealing to them (after three holes of behavior they later were very embarrassed by) that there is more to life than chasing a dimpled spheroid around a landscaped grass patch, more uplifting activities to be involved in that telling dirty jokes or coping with hangovers, and there are decisions far more important to make than whether to use a 9-iron or a pitching wedge when you're fifty yards away from the green.

For the man whose wife of more than thirty five years had just gone on to be with the Lord in glory, God put a smile on his face this week as he focused his attention on the wonderful blessing she was now experiencing in God's presence and how she was singing with His angels in heaven, free of pain, and seeing the Lord face to face.

And, for the twenty young women willing to attend a prison Bible Study, God assured them this week of His undying love, His willingness to forgive and to give second and third and hundredth chances, and that God can cleanse even the dirtiest heart and foulest mouth because of the shed blood of Jesus.

In short, the circumstances were different, but the message was the same…

God loves you and He is THE answer you've been looking for.

To the reader…
I want to assure you too that whatever circumstance you're in, Jesus is THE answer to your questions, and your way through the problems.

To the Lord…
Thank You for the simple but amazing truth…You love even me!

BAPTIZED IN THE JORDAN

If all goes as planned...

I'm getting baptized today!

"What?! We thought you were already baptized, pastor!"
Well, yes, I was baptized, just as one should be, within days of declaring publicly how I had received Jesus as my personal Lord and Savior. In my case I was nine years old and living in Kansas City, Missouri at the time.

However, as baptism is an opportunity to declare to the world your love and commitment to the Lord, I have chosen to do so AGAIN today and will also be baptizing others in our group touring the Holy Land right now.

And I'm doing it where Jesus was baptized...in the Jordan River!

In addition to the baptisms, today our group itinerary includes a boat ride on the Sea of Galilee, a tour up to the lifted-up fortress of Masada, and, later this evening we'll get to "float" on the salt water of the Dead Sea.

The beautiful Jordan River valley with the flowing water of the Jordan affords a great contrast with the Dead Sea. It's especially amazing when you realize that the very water that makes the Jordan River valley be so ALIVE and GREEN flows into the Salt Sea, in which NOTHING can live...hence the name, "Dead Sea." In fact, the salt content of the Dead Sea is so high that you cannot drown, you can only float on top of the incredible mass of "goo."

What could cause such a drastic contrast? Well, it's simple actually: the water flows INTO the Dead Sea but there is NO OUTLET for it to pass through. Consequently, the water stagnates and is unfit for living creatures.

The same is true in the life of a Christian.

If we only "take in" information from Bible Study lessons, sermons, answered prayers, if we only "receive" God's love but never "let it out" by expressing God's amazing gospel and the truths He reveals to us each day, we become "Dead Sea Christians"—possessing plenty of the "salt of the earth," but NOT producing new life.

Today I invite you to "let it out."

Let others know of your love and commitment to the Lord.
It can be as simple as talking to your next-door neighbor or others whom you have yet to tell about the Lord, and "letting it out" by letting them know.
And, if you know the Lord but haven't yet been baptized, I invite you to do what I'm doing today, and be baptized as a testimony of your love and commitment to the Lord.

To the reader…
    Are you allowing God's Spirit to flow like Living Water through you and produce healthy fruit in your life? If not, my prayer for you is you will let go and let Him flow.

To the Lord…
    While I'm in the Jordan River today, I'll be thanking You for flowing through me.

NO DUTCH TREAT

The fine was $4,500, and there's a larger fine possible if she refuses to behave in compliance with the government's demands.

Wow! To face that stiff penalty she must have committed a pretty dastardly deed, huh? Maybe a heinous murder, complete with chainsaw, perhaps?

Wrong.

Actually her "crime" was one of spelling!

This past week the Danish government fined a mother $4,500 for spelling her son's name with too many "ph"-es! It seems her choice of spelling is not on the "approved list" of names registered with the government of Denmark.

She chose to spell her son's name, "Christophpher," using one extra "ph," and for that "crime" she was fined and threatened with imprisonment if she does not change her spelling within thirty days. Pretty dumb, huh?

Well, unfortunate as it might be...

Denmark isn't the only place where "legalism" reigns.

Its alive...and SICK...in America too—many times even in her churches!

During this very season when we celebrate the birth of Jesus who came "to set free the captives" and to take the burden of those who are heavy-laden, there are some (well-meaning as they might be) who wrongly set themselves up as the legal and/or moral "watchdogs" over us all. They are convinced that only THEIR stands are "acceptable," and woe to anyone who dares cross a "t" or dot an "I" in a different way from them!

OBSERVATIONS FROM THE WEIRD BEARDED GUY

Woe to anyone, they might say, who dares read from a Bible translation that isn't the "authorized" version (although the "authorized" version simply meant King James of England in 1611 "authorized" scholars to translate the Latin Vulgate into English, now dubbed "the King's English"). Interestingly, the more modern translations translated straight from the Hebrew and Greek and have correctly translated words as they are used now rather than how their meanings were understood in 1611.

Woe, some of these legalists say, to any church who sings praise songs rather than hymns only (even though the Bible expressly tells us to worship the Lord with NEW songs), or woe to anyone who changes the "acceptable" order of worship services, woe to any church with a different-from-the-"acceptable" starting or ending time of their services, or woe to anyone who…and from there the list has included at one time or another and in one group or another the following "no-o's": ladies wearing too much make-up or sporting an improper skirt hem-length, men with facial hair, anyone wearing brightly-colored clothing or jewelry, anyone who might display a painting of Jesus, or celebrates any kind of holiday, any preacher whose sermon lasts past noon, etc., etc., etc.

Now, in Denmark, it's spelling that's the issue.

PPPLLLEEEASE! Let's stop the insanity!

To the reader…

The truth is…Jesus came to set you free. God's into grace rather than legalism.

Joy to the world! The Lord is come!

To the Lord…

I want to PRPRPRPRPRPRAISE Your name, Lord, for Your grace and mercy.

TWELVE PARTRIDGES AND TWELVE PEAR TREES

You know how it goes: "Four calling birds, three French hens, two turtle doves, and a partridge in a pear tree." What you might not know, though, is that an expensive set of gifts these items turn out to be.

Recently, someone in New York (someone with entirely too much time on his hands) decided to investigate it for comparison of this year's economy vs. last year's economy, so the cost was revealed in today's dollars.

Based on union-scale wages for the musicians (pipers, drummers) and dancers (lords o' leaping, ladies dancing), minimum wage for the maids o' milking, the current price of gold for the rings, the going price for the various birds, and the orchard price of a pear tree, the LAST DAY total (just for the 12th day gifts, which, jogging your memory you might recall includes 12 lords o' leaping, 11 pipers piping, 10 drummers drumming, nine ladies dancing, 8 maids o' milking, 7 swans a-swimming, 6 geese a-laying, 5 golden rings, 4 calling birds, 3 French hens, 2 turtle doves, and a partridge in a pear tree) came to more than $15,000,000.

And, if you added up ALL the days' totals (which means your true love would have given to you 12 lords, 22 pipers, 30 drummers, 36 dancing ladies, 40 maids, 42 swans, 42 geese, 40 gold rings, 36 calling birds, 30 French hens, 22 doves, 12 partridges, and 12 pear trees), the grand total becomes more than $62,000,000!

Yet, it doesn't necessarily mean your "true love" REALLY loves you.

It simply means that your true love has a lot of spendable income. True love is always demonstrated in giving, but giving isn't always due to love—sometimes it's for less-than-honorable reasons, like power or manipulation, pride or intimidation, or an attempt to "purchase" a person's affections. That's why the best gifts aren't necessarily purchased with lots of cash, but come FROM THE HEART.

To the reader...
This Christmas I encourage you to remember these three things:
a) In terms of cash, Jesus' birth did cost Joseph and Mary an amount of it—they left Nazareth for Bethlehem, stayed there several months, then left and stayed in Egypt for another period of months, maybe as many as two years before they finally returned to Nazareth. Certainly there were some expenses incurred, but the greatest gift, the greatest cost was in their time, their hearts and their willingness to be used of God. And God honored their gifts.

b) The greatest gift ever given was given by God, the Father, when He gave His only begotten Son, Jesus. There is no way to put a monetary price on such a gift, and yet it will cost you your very life if our refuse to receive it.

c) This Christmas, why not give the Lord what He truly desires...the same that Mary and Joseph gave Him: your availability for God to work through you. That's a whole lot better than a partridge, don't you think?

To the Lord...
I want to be a-leaping in service to You.
Anything else is simply "for the birds."

'TWAS THE NIGHT BEFORE CHRISTMAS

They were poor. They had very few possessions, and his line of work as a carpenter was one with great seasonal fluctuations—sometimes plenty of work, sometimes none.

She was young—many felt she was too young.

And although she was in a "committed" relationship, she was unmarried. Talk in the community was already heating up, side glances were being cast her way and also at her husband-to-be and their families, the kind of talk and scorn that wouldn't let up. Her family's reputation was at stake. Her own reputation and that of her husband-to-be were in many ways already shattered. He obviously cared a great deal about her, but did he care enough to endure the shunning both they AND the child would have to deal with for the rest of their lives?

As the pressure increased, she left town for several months, staying with a relative in a nearby city, an aunt who was also expecting a child, a relative she could talk to freely concerning hard decisions she needed to make.

Having decided, and as the time was quickly approaching for her to give birth, her fiancee helped her go to a small town many miles away—an isolated little village where no one knew her, and there she did what many believed was the wisest "choice"—she had an abortion.

Sadly, this is the choice so many have chosen.
However, Mary and Joseph made the TOUCH choice—for LIFE.

Needless to say, Jesus' birth was miraculous—He was born of a virgin. As a result, He was born without a sin nature.

He was born into a world of which He had personally created everything in it.

His birth was foretold by Old Testament prophets, heralded by multitudes of angels, announced by a special heavenly "beacon" that guided visitors from the East to Him, announced to shepherds, told to the king, revealed to two elderly people of faith in the temple, and was the focus of the greatest verse in the Bible, John 3:16—"For God so loved the world, that He gave His only begotten Son."

And yet, sometimes we as Baptists and other non-Catholics too, perhaps out of a knee jerk reaction to our Catholic friends' tendency to over-emphasize the role of Mary in Jesus' life and ministry, tend to overlook entirely the incredible surrender and sacrifice shown by Mary AND by Joseph in following through with their commitment to bringing Jesus into the world and serving as His earthly parents.

Even BEFORE Jesus proclaimed the Gospel message He was already "despised and rejected of men"—right from the very beginning due to the circumstances of His birth.

Still, Mary allowed herself to become the "hand-maiden of God," and Joseph quietly gave earthly leadership to the child Jesus so the world know His real Father—OUR Father, Who art in heaven.

Thank you, Mary and Joseph, for "carrying through" your commitment.

While Santa and Rudolph may get the headlines tonight, your devotion was the vessel God chose to truly "deliver" the greatest gift of all to ALL the world.

On, Mary! On, Joseph! On, donkey! On, Jesus!

To the reader…

Tonight, on Christmas Eve, remember that God gave His only begotten Son…to you…to demonstrate His love for you by sending His Son to the earth…to be born in Bethlehem, but also to die in Jerusalem.

I invite you to unwrap that package and receive it as the Father intended…by faith and with gratitude.

The only appropriate gift you can give Him in return is to give Him the right to be Lord of your life. Will you do it?

To the Lord…
I thank You that Your blood was shed to wash away, wash away, wash away ALL…my sin!

AN EPILOGUE

Leon Russell wrote it. Then he and Donny Hathaway and The Carpenters and Andy Williams, and who knows who else, recorded it.

The title of the song: "A Song For You."

The poignant lyrics declare, "I've acted out my life in stages, with ten thousand people watching, but we're alone now and I'm singing this song for you."[19]

I very much relate to those lyrics. I didn't need to live in a glass house, because when you're in "the ministry," you end up living your life with everyone watching.

And, as you go through the normal stages of life, you do so with ten thousand people watching, and one hundred thousand people ready to criticize and advise you.

So, as a college student falling in and out and back in love again for keeps; as a newlywed working with young people and college students and parents; as a husband seeking to love and support the wonderful woman God brought into my life; as an in-law "fitting in" to an extended family; as a first time dad serving in a church full of grandmas and older dads; as a conference leader meeting hundreds of new people every day while your wife and family are back home coping without you being at home in the evenings; as a college professor with students looking up to you and, to some degree, fearing you; as a sports chaplain striving to provide spiritual encouragement while still remaining neutral in sporting events; as a pastor supervising a staff, providing counseling, presiding at weddings and funerals, visiting folk in hospitals and institutions; as a preacher seeking to instruct and inspire; as a son seeking to assist and care for my wonderful parents as they reach their "golden ages"; and as a church planter seeking to "birth" a new congregation; I have lived my life in stages, and more than ten thousand people have been watching all along.

OBSERVATIONS FROM THE WEIRD BEARDED GUY

In writing this book I've sought to "open up" and offer my own observations as events around me have unfolded. And, unashamedly, I have attempted to pass along what I believe is the "secret" to a meaningful and enjoyable life: a personal relationship with Jesus Christ.

You see, I don't proclaim Jesus to you because I'm a preacher, I do so because I am a satisfied customer.

So, in bringing the book to a close, I offer these final observations:
    a) Yes, I'm a guy.

        I really had no choice about that one, but I like being one.
    b) Yes, I've got a beard.

        Actually it's now a goatee, and it's there by my choice. I have found that it helps cover a multitude of chins, and has opened some doors for me in gaining a more receptive audience with teenagers and young adults along the way.

    c) And, yes, I'm weird.

        Again, that's by choice. I don't mean I'm a wacko, I'm not someone you would need to be afraid of if I were to ride on the same subway car as yours. But my sense of humor is a little off the wall; I've discovered funny things in nearly every event, and delight in the uniqueness of every individual. I have no doubt that God has a sense of humor because I've closely observed the people He has created and have found them to be delightfully humorous…that is, when they don't take themselves too seriously.

To the reader…

It is my fervent prayer that you will "take a chance" and receive Jesus by faith as your own Savior and Lord. All the observations, all the writing will be worth it to me if you will simply give Him an honest look.

To the Lord…

Thank You for loving me throughout all the stages and while I've stood on thousands of stages over the years.

We're not alone now, Lord, but I wrote this book for You.

NOTES

[1] Charles Swindoll, Starting Over. (Portland, Oregon: Multnomah Press), 1983.
[2] Ibid.
[3] The Congressional Record, September 19, 1985.
[4] Led Zeppelin, "Stairway To Heaven," Led Zepellin IV. Atlantic Records, 1971.
[5] Martha and the Vandellas, "Heat Wave," Heat Wave. Motown Records, 1963.
[6] Henry Beard and Christopher Cerf, The Official Politically Correct Dictionary and Handbook. (New York: Villard Books), 1983.

[7] Ibid.
[8] Paramount Pictures, Forrest Gump, 1994.

[9] Robert McNamara, In Retrospect: The Tragedy and Lessons Of Vietnam. (New York: Times Books), 1995.

[10] "Struck Out," The Winston Salem Journal, May 22, 1995.
[11] William P. Merrill, William H. Walter, "Rise Up, O Men Of God," Hymnal With Tunes Old and New. Published by F. J. Huntington, 1872.

[12] Scott O'Grady, Michael French, Basher Five-Two. (New York: Random House Children's Books), 1998.

[13] Time Magazine, September 12, 1969.

[14] Ibid.

OBSERVATIONS FROM THE WEIRD BEARDED GUY

[15] Dan Franklin, "1994 In Review: Orange Country Gets a Reputation," The Orange County Register. January 1, 1995.

[16] Lyrics by J. B. F. Wright, "Precious Memories, How They Linger," 1925.

[17] "Streets Of Laredo" a.k.a. "The Cowboy's Lament," A Cowboy Traditional and American Folksong, origin unclear.

[18] Smothers Brothers, "Laredo," The Two Sides of the Smothers Brothers, Mercury Records, 1962.

[19] Leon Russell, "A Song For You," Leon Russell, DCC Records, 1970.

Also available from PublishAmerica

SLEEP TIGHT
by Barbara Wagner

Attractive Caryl Stewart, a western artist, has inherited a fortune and fallen in love with David Eagle, the confident and sensual man of her dreams. When her flamboyant, oil-rich great-aunt, Savannah Buckman, dies, the young redhead travels from Scottsdale, Arizona, to manage her great-aunt's estate in upscale Winter Park near Oklahoma City. After a disturbing secret from Savannah's past is revealed and a manipulative friend, almost Caryl's exact twin, becomes the third victim, Caryl knows she is the target of a cunning killer, an unknown murderer who is slowly going insane. Tormented by Oklahoma wind and trapped in the eerie atmosphere of a mysterious mansion, she struggles to escape from a maze of terror, revenge and murder. When her Native American lover is accused, Caryl makes a startling discovery and a cruel psychopath prepares to combine her death with his pleasure.

Paperback, 289 pages
6" x 9"
ISBN 1-60610-096-3

About the author:

Both a writer and an artist, Barbara Wagner lives with her husband in a suburb of Kansas City close to their grown children. She grew up in Oklahoma, has a degree in fine art from the University of Oklahoma, and studied creative writing at Butler University in Indianapolis. An award-winning artist, her work was marketed in Scottsdale, Arizona, for many years. Though *Sleep Tight* is entirely a work of fiction, the artistic life of the novel's protagonist, Caryl Stewart, is drawn from Barbara's own experience and adds a strong framework to the suspenseful story.

Available to all bookstores nationwide.
www.publishamerica.com

Also available from PublishAmerica

EMILLEE KART AND THE SEVEN SAVING SIGNS
THE TALE OF BEASLEY'S BONNET

by Vanessa Wheeler

From the minute she met her eccentric missionary aunt, Emillee Kart's life would never be the same. During their first lunch at the Butterfly Café, Emillee is inducted into a secret club known as the Monarch's Army; minutes later she is running for her life. Not only is Emillee launched into an age-old battle between the Skywalkers and the Hexiums, she may very well be the key to saving the Earthtreadors. Twelve years ago, on the day Emillee was born, a prophecy spread throughout the land of a child that would turn the tide of the battle. Five children were born on that day; two have disappeared. The Hexiums will stop at nothing to eliminate any threat to their victory. Emillee needs to learn who she is in order to help uncover the clues that will bring the Skywalkers closer to their goal.

Paperback, 202 pages
5.5" x 8.5"
ISBN 1-4241-8597-1

About the author:

Love of fantasy combined with spiritual conviction guided this mother of three to spin this faith-based tale. Joanne Strobel-Cort, born in Bethlehem, Pennsylvania, now lives in Summit, New Jersey, with her husband and three children. She works on Wall Street and is a committed Sunday school teacher who relies on faith to meet the challenges of each day.

Available to all bookstores nationwide.
www.publishamerica.com

Also available from PublishAmerica

Dovie
A Tribute Written by Her Son

by Ken Eichler

My first recollections of my life was when I had just turned three. I was in an orphanage and my mama was crying. I didn't know why. She was just crying and I wanted her to feel better. As I grew a little older in the orphanage, I realized what it was all about. I had become three and the rules were that a child could no longer stay in the room with their mother after that. They had to be transferred to a dormitory with other children of about the same age and sex. I believe that was when my mama firmly made up her mind to leave the orphanage to seek a new husband and a new home where we could all live together again. It didn't exactly work out that way and it was a crushing blow to Mama. But that had become the norm for my mama and grandparents. They all had lived their lives from birth in dirty, dark and dangerous mining camps, going through one mine explosion that killed 30 of their friends and acquaintances. And shortly thereafter, losing several loved ones to a national and worldwide devastating disease. And traumatic deaths followed my mama and grandma throughout their lives, even my daddy, who died at the age of 40 of bee stings that left my mama with six small children, including me at the age of three weeks. But we had a Savior that led us to the greatest fraternal organizations in the world, and still the greatest ones in existence today—The Masonic Fraternity and The Order of the Eastern Star. A large part of my story deals with our lives and experiences in the Home they built for us, as well as the lives and experiences of hundreds more who came there to live with us. My mama and my grandma spent almost a lifetime in abject poverty and grief when, except for fate, they would have been among the wealthy and aristocratic families in Birmingham and Jefferson County. I have often wondered: what, exactly, went wrong?

Paperback, 142 pages
5.5" x 8.5"
ISBN 1-60672-171-2

Available to all bookstores nationwide.
www.publishamerica.com

Also available from PublishAmerica

CAUGHT MIDSTREAM
by Uta Christensen

In *Caught Midstream*, Janos, a successful executive, reveals the untold experiences of his youth quite unexpectedly to Sparrow—a young woman he is attracted to. She is allowed to relive his epic journey and becomes drawn into an unnerving yet moving tapestry of travails and extraordinary events that take place in prisoner-of-war camps deep within Russia. Taken by force at age sixteen from the protective circle of his family in Germany, Janos is tossed into the cataclysmic, last-gasp efforts of World War II. His journey takes him to a place of darkness, where he lives through a near-death experience and goes through physical and emotional starvation, hard labor, and ostracism; yet it also carries him into unlikely places and relationships where friendship, compassion, healing, mentoring, and love can, amazingly, still flourish. As the story unfolds, Janos's journey accelerates from adolescence into manhood. Almost miraculously, Janos survives while vast numbers of his co-travelers perish.

Paperback, 271 pages
6" x 9"
ISBN 1-4241-0967-1

About the author:

Born in Germany, Uta Christensen spent years in Ireland, New Zealand, and Australia but settled permanently in California. Holding a B.A. in English and German literature, she taught English at a community college and was an administrative analyst at the University of California. Her first book, her father's memoir, was published in Germany.

Available to all bookstores nationwide.
www.publishamerica.com